DOG FOX FIELD

Les Murray

DOG FOX FIELD

CARCANET

To the glory of God

First published in Great Britain in 1991 by
Carcanet Press Limited
208–212 Corn Exchange Buildings
Manchester M4 3BQ

Published in Australia by Collins/Angus & Robertson Publishers

British Library Cataloguing in Publication Data
Murray, Les A. (Les Allan)
Dog fox field.
1. Title
821

ISBN 0-85635-950-5

The Publisher acknowledges financial assistance from
the Arts Council of Great Britain

Printed in England by SRP Ltd., Exeter

CONTENTS

ACKNOWLEDGEMENTS

Poems in this book have been published in the ABC
Bicentennial anthology *The Tin Wash Dish*, the *Adelaide
Review*, the *Age*, *Antipodes*, *Australian Cultural History*,
Australian Way, the *Australian*, *Canberra Times*, *Eremos
Newsletter*, the *Formalist*, *Grand Street*, *Great Lakes Advocate*, the
Humorist, *Island*, *Landfall*, *London Review of Books*, *Mattara
Anthology 1988*, *Meanjin*, *Mercedes*, *New Republic*, *New Welsh
Review*, *Paris Review*, *Poetry Australia*, *Poetry Ireland Review*,
Poetry Review, *Poetry Kanto* (Japan), *Quadrant*, *St Marks
Review*, *Scripsi*, *Southerly*, *Sport* (NZ), *Sydney Morning Herald*,
Sydney Review, *Trucking Life*, *Verse*, the *Warringah Book*,
Westerly, *Word International* and *Yale Review*. Four of the
poems also appeared in *The Idyll Wheel*, a limited edition book
published by Officina Brindabella, Canberra 1989, and many
were broadcast by the ABC, BBC, NZBC, RTÉ (Ireland),
Radio 2GB, Channels 7 and 9 (Sydney), 2BOB-FM and others.
For support and hospitality during the years when these
poems were being written, I am grateful to the Literary Arts
Board of the Australia Council, to Paul Keating MHR, and to
innumerable friends and institutions at home and overseas.

The Transposition of Clermont

After the Big Flood, we elected
to move our small timber city
from the dangerous beauty of the river
and its fringed lagoons
since both had risen to destroy us.

Many buildings went stacked on wagons
but more were towed entire
in strained stateliness, with a long groyning sound,
up timber by traction engines.

Each moved singly. Life went on round them;
in them, at points of rest.
Guests at breakfast in the Royal Hotel, facing
now the saddlery, now the Town Hall.

We drank in the canted Freemasons
and the progressive Shamrock, but really
all pubs were the Exchange. Relativities
interchanged our world like a chess game:

butcher occluded baker, the police
eclipsed both brothels, the dance hall
sashayed around the Temperance Hall,
front doors sniffed rear, and thoughtfully ground on.

Certain houses burst, and vanished.
One wept its windows, one trailed mementoes up the street.
A taut chain suddenly parted and scythed down
horses and a verandah. Weed-edged black rectangles
in exploded gardens yielded sovereigns and spoons.

That ascent of working architecture
onto the pegged plateau was a children's crusade
with lines stretching down to us.

Everything standing in its wrong accustomed place.
My generation's memories are intricately transposed:

butcher occluding dance music, the police
eclipsed by opportunity, brothels sashaying royally
and, riding sidesaddle up shined skids, the Town Hall.
Excited, we would meet on streets that stayed immutable

sometimes for weeks; from irrecoverable corners
and alleys already widening, we'd look
back down at our new graves and childhood gardens,
the odd house at anchor for a quick tomato season
and the swaying nailed hull of a church going on before us.

And many allotments left unbought, or for expansion
never filled up, above, as they hadn't below.
What was town, what was country stayed elusive
as we saw it always does, in the bush,
what is waste, what is space, what is land.

Feb

Seedy drytime Feb,
lightning between its teeth,
all its plants pot-bound.

Inside enamelled rims
dams shrink their mirroring shields,
baking the waterlilies.

Days stacked like clay pigeons
squeezed from dust and sweat.
Two cultures: sun and shade.

Days dazed with actuality
like a bottle shot
sniping fruit off twigs,

by afternoon, portentous
with whole cloud-Atlantics
that rain fifteen drops.

Beetroot and iron butter,
bread staled by the fan,
cold chook: that's lunch with Feb.

Weedy drymouth Feb, first cousin of scorched creek stones,
of barbed wire across gaunt gullies, bringer of soldered
death-freckles to the backs of farmers' hands. The mite-struck

foal rattles her itch on fence wires, like her mother
and scraped hill pastures are grazed back to their charred
bulldozer stitchings. Dogs nip themselves under the tractor

of needy Feb, who waits for the raw eel-perfume
of the first real rain's pheromones, the magic rain-on-dust
sexual scent of Time itself, philtre of all native beings —

3

Lanky cornhusk Feb,
drilling the red-faced
battalions of tomatoes

through the grader's slots:
harvest out of bareness,
that semidesert mode.

Worn grasshopper month
suddenly void of children;
days tucking their tips in

with blackberry seeds to spit
and all of life root-bound;
stringy dryland Feb.

Masculeene, Cried the Bulls

Bang! it was autumn
right on the first of the month,
cool overcast after scorchers
and next day it poured.

Four and a half inches
of rise in the dams, of wet in garden soil:
we know how long you were, rain,
four and a half deep inches.

As fresh green abolished
this summer's only white-blonde month
the first autumnal scents
were ginger and belladonna

and as beds resumed their blankets
at the mopoke hour, bulls sang.
Among cattle, the more masculine
the higher the voice is pitched.

Our pumpkins took
first prize at Nabiac Show,
where a horse named Danielle
pirouetted, and posed on a tub,

and men raced through solid timber
backwards, with aimed steel strides,
and we met the Anglo-Nubian
tree-climbing goat, maker of,

and sheep of, the desert.
This was the weekend after clocks
jerked the sun an hour forward,
and all the time, leafage

of various winebottle colour
sprouted on the roses and lemon trees
and dew twinkled for longer
on the lengthening paddocks.

The Idyll Wheel

And so we've come right round the sun
to April again. It's unique again
like each month, each year. Much less of summer
reached April this year. Yet grass burgeoned after Easter
and fenced cultivations rug up, blue and tan.

The sliding fit of month to season
sees more frogs bronze-backed now than green
and old fruit trees declare themselves
along creekbanks in russet and fawn
like cedars long ago spied from a mountain.

The seasons used to blur, or so we dream,
on the wheel of an idyll, before we came.
An idle wheel, we said, and lashed
the years to make them a driving wheel.
Idylls were idols, thefts of time.

But an idyll of land had brought us here
in ships from the far side of the year.
In the evening of our youth we'd stand
in good broad cloth, the spokes of one hand
on our belly, beneath oaks of a vast idea,

for *idyll* derives from *eidos*, form.
It too shapes cityscape and farm.
And the farms once made, they live by touches,
a stump burning, scooped dam, new wire stitches
and unstated idylls had driving to and from.

So, into blue dimensionless as an ideal
with a Y-tipped prop our neighbour hoists the unreal
statures, flat and wet, of her whole family
for her glance and the warm sun to re-fill
above the pleats and rare flickers of their hill
where her old father tinily moves, keeping busy.
The idyll wheel is the working wheel.

The Fall of Aphrodite Street

So it's back to window shopping
on Aphrodite Street
for the apples are stacked and juicy
but some are death to eat.

For just one generation
the plateglass turned to air —
when you look for that generation
half of it isn't there.

An ugliness of spirit
leered like a hunting dog
over the world. Now it snarls and whines
at its fleshly analogue.

What pleased it made it angry:
scholars Score and Flaunt and Scene
taught that everything outstanding
was knobs on a skin machine.

Purer grades of this metaphysic
were sold out of parked cars
down alleys where people paired or reeled
like desperate swastikas.

Age, spirit, kindness, all were taunts;
grace was enslaved to meat.
You never were mugged till you were mugged
on Aphrodite Street.

God help the millions that street killed
and those it sickened too,
when it was built past every house
and often bulldozed through.

Apples still swell, but more and more
are literal death to eat
and it's back to window shopping
on Aphrodite Street.

Two Rains

Our farm is in the patched blue overlap
between Queensland rain and Victorian rain
(and of two-faced droughts like a dustbowl tap).

The southerly rain is skimmed and curled
off the Roaring Forties' circuit of the world.
It is our chased Victorian silver

and makes wintry asphalt hurry on the spot
or pauses to a vague speed in the air,
whereas, lightning-brewed in a vast coral pot

the tropical weather disgorges its lot
in days of enveloping floodtime blast
towering and warm as a Papuan forest,

a rain you can sweat in, it steams in the sun
like a hard-ridden horse, while southern rain's absorbed
like a cool, fake-colloquial, drawn out lesson.

To the Soviet Americans

The working class, the working class,
it is too radiant to see through.
More claim to come from the working class
than admit they do.

Between syruping mailed brutes in flattery
and translating the world into litmag terms
those equivalent modes of poetry
there comes this love of the working class

who never set out to be a class
or the subject forever of exams
they're not allowed to take or pass
or else they're no longer the working class,

and in the forest, a working man
must say, *Watch out for the ones in jeans*
who'll stop you smoking and stop you working:
I call them the Soviet Americans.

I used to have work and a family here
but both them have shot through.
Now that trees belong to the working class
I don't suppose I do.

Low Down Sandcastle Blues

You can't have everything, I said as we drank tea.
No, you can't have everything. And I sipped my tea.
   You can't have anything, my friend answered me.

Yes, I've wrestled with an angel: there is no other kind.
I wrestled with an angel: that wrestling's the only kind.
   Any easier wrestling finally sends you blind.

Trouble's a stray dog that's mighty hard to lose:
if he latches on to you, he's mighty hard to lose
   but not even a dog joins in when you sing the blues.

A man told me I've no right to what I need.
He told me Oh yes, I've no right to what I need.
   He had all his rights and quivered under them like a reed.

If you've got the gift of seeing things from both sides
— it's an angel-wound, that curse of seeing things from both
   sides —
   then police beat you up in a sandcastle built between tides:

Preface to The Idyll Wheel

An east-running valley where two hooded creeks make
    junction
and two snoring roads make a rainguttered cross of function:

there, each hamlet of house-and-sheds stands connected and
    alone
and the chimneys of old houses are square bottles cut from
    iron.

Gum forest is a solid blue cloud on the hills to the south
and bladygrass and chain rust round its every wheeltracked
    mouth.

Being back home there, where I am all my ages,
I wanted to trace a year through all its stages.

I would start after summer, to catch a subtly vernal effect
(April is also when I conceived the project).

At one poem per month, it would take a baker's dozen
to accommodate the stretch and overlap of season

into season, in any single year —
and to be real, the year had to be particular

since this wasn't to be a cyclic calendar
of miniature peasantry painted as for a proprietor.

No one can own all Bunyah. Names shouted over coal-oil
    lamps
cling to their paddocks. Bees and dingoes tax the cattlecamps.

As forefather Hesiod may have learned, too, by this time,
things don't recur precisely, on the sacred earth: they rhyme.

To illuminate one year on that known ground
would also draw light from the many gone underground

with steel wedges and glass and the forty thousand days lost or
worked, daylight to dark, there between Forster and
Gloucester.

So: as grass tips turn maroon in a further winter
I present how time revolved through the spiral of a year

average, says experience, in erosions and deposit of seeds.
I thank Rosalind Atkins, whose burin opens up further leads

into the heart of it, making the more exquisite lines —
and I thank Alec Bolton for a book that dresses ours to the
nines.

The Emerald Dove

We ought to hang cutout hawk shapes
in our windows. Birds hard driven
by a predator, or maddened by a mirrored rival
too often die zonk against the panes'
invisible sheer, or stagger away from
the blind full stop in the air.
It was different with the emerald dove.
In at an open sash, a pair

sheered, missile, in a punch of energy,
one jinking on through farther doors, one
thrown, panicked by that rectangular wrong copse, braked
like a bullet in blood, a full-on splat of wings
like a vaulter between shoulders, blazed and calliper,
ashriek out of jagbeaked fixe fury, swatting wind,
lights, keepsakes, panes, then at the in window out, gone.
A sparrowhawk, by the cirrus feathering.

The other, tracked down in a farther room
clinging to a bedhead, was the emerald dove,
a rainforest bird, flashed in beyond its world
of lice, sudden death and tree seeds. Pigeon-like,
only its eye and neck in liquid motion,
there, as much beyond us as beyond
itself, it perched, barefoot in silks
like a prince of Sukhothai, above the reading lamps and
    cotton-buds.

Modest-sized as a writing hand, mushroom fawn
apart from its paua casque, those viridescent closed wings,
it was an emerald Levite in that bedroom
which the memory of it was going to bless for years
despite topping our ordinary happiness, as beauty
makes background of all around it. Levite too

in the question it posed: sanctuary without transformation,
which is, how we might be,

plunged out of our contentment into evolved strange heaven,
where the need to own or mate with or eat the beautiful
was bygone as poverty,
and we were incomprehensibly, in our exhaustion,
treasured, cooed at, then softly left alone
among vast crumples, verticals, refracting air,
our way home barred by mirrors, our splendour unmanifest
to us now, a small wild person, with no idea of peace.

Cave Divers Near Mount Gambier

Chenille-skinned people are counting under the countryside
on resurrections by truck light off among the pines.

Here in the first paddocks, where winter comes ashore,
mild duckweed ponds are skylights of a filled kingdom

and what their gaze absorbs may float up districts away.
White men with scorches of hair approach that water,

zip into black, upturn large flap feet and free-fall
away, their mouths crammed full. Crystalline polyps

of their breathing blossom for a while, as they disturb
algal screens, extinct kangaroos, eels of liquorice colour

then, with the portable greening stars they carry under,
these vanish, as the divers undergo tight anti-births

into the vaults and profound domes of the limestone.
Here, approaching the heart of the poem they embody

and thereby make the gliding cavern-world embody,
they have to keep time with themselves, and be dull often

with its daylight logic — since to dream it fully
might leave them asprawl on the void clang of their tanks,

their faceplates glazing an unfocussed dreadful portrait
at the apex of a steeple that does not reach the day.

The Tin Wash Dish

Lank poverty, dank poverty,
its pants wear through at fork and knee.
It warms its hands over burning shames,
refers to its fate as Them and He
and delights in things by their hard names:
rag and toejam, feed and paw —
don't guts that down, there ain't no more!
Dank poverty, rank poverty,
it hums with a grim fidelity
like wood-rot with a hint of orifice,
wet newspaper jammed in the gaps of artifice,
and disgusts us into fierce loyalty.
It's never the fault of those you love:
poverty comes down from above.
Let it dance chairs and smash the door,
it arises from all that went before
and every outsider's the enemy —
Jesus Christ turned this over with his stick
and knights and philosophers truned it back.
Rank poverty, lank poverty,
chafe in its crotch and sores in its hair,
still a window's clean if it's made of air
and not webbed silver like a sleeve.
Watch out if this does well at school
and has to leave and longs to leave:
someone, sometime, will have to pay.
Lank poverty, dank poverty,
the cornbag quilt breeds such loyalty.
Shave with toilet soap, run to flesh,
astound the nation, run the army,
still you wait for the day you'll be sent back
where books or toys on the floor are rubbish
and no one's allowed to come and play
because home calls itself a shack
and hot water crinkles in the tin wash dish.

The Inverse Transports

Two hundred years, and the bars
reappear on more and more windows;
more people have a special number to ring.
This started with furious strange Christians:
they would have all things in common,
have morals superseded by love —
truth and Christ they rejected scornfully.

More people sell and move to the country.
The bush becomes their civil city.
What do they do there? Some make quilts
sewing worn and washed banknotes together.
What romantic legends do they hear there?
Tales of lineage, and of terrible accidents:
the rearing tractor, the sawmills' bloody moons.

Accident is the tiger of the country,
but fairytale is a reserve, for those rich only
in that and fifty thousand years here.
The incomers will acquire those fifty thousand
years too, though. Thousands of anything
draw them. They discovered thousands,
even these. Which they offer now, for settlement.

Has the nation been a poem or an accident?
And which should it be? America, and the Soviets
and the First and Third Reich were poems.
Two others, quite different, have been Rome's.
We've been through some bloody British stanzas
and some local stanzas where "pelf"
was the rhyme for "self" — and some about police,

refuge, ballots, space, the Fair Go and peace.
Many strain now to compose a National Purpose,
some fear its enforcement. Free people take liberties:

inspired government takes liberty itself.
Takes it where, court to parliament to bureaucracy
to big union to gaol, an agreed atmosphere
endures, that's dealt with God and democracy.

Inside convict ships that Christ's grace inverted
hanging chains end in lights. Congregations
approach the classless there. But the ships are being buried
in tipped dirt. Half the media denies
it's happening, and the other half justifies
this live burial — and the worshippers divide likewise
in their views of the sliding waves of garbage

in which their ships welter and rise
beneath towers with the lyric sheen of heroin
that reach skyward out of the paradox
that expression and achievement are the Prize
and at the same time are indefensible privilege.
Two hundred years, and the bars
appear on more and more windows.

The Billions

At the whizz of a door screen
moorhens picking through our garden
make it by a squeak into the dam
and breasting the algal water

resume their gait and pace on
submerged spectral feet, and they nod
like that half-filled Coke bottle
we saw in the infant river

as it came to its affliction
in the skinny rapids. There
it made a host of dinky bows,
jinked, spun and signalled

till it was in the calm again.
Riding wet in a wide reach of glare
it made us think of icebergs
towed to a desert harbour

for drink and irrigation,
stranded incongruous wet mountains
that destroy the settled scale there,
but, imported in a billion pieces

that's how the Coke world is.
And though, as immemorially,
all our dream-ships come,
and go, to Cervix Paradise,

now when day puts us ashore
we walk on gritty ice
in wideawake cities
with tower flats and smog horizon

and there we work, illusionless,
scared lest *live* rhyme with *naive*
till the evening lights come on.
That's the Enlightenment: Surface Paradise.

It cures symptoms, and is fun,
but almost any warmth makes floes
those caught on them must defend
as the inner fields expand,

floes with edges like a billion.
Strange, that wanting to believe
humans could fully awaken
should take away the land.

The Narrabri Reservation

On the road to the Nandewars
there was a slab of dead
enfolded in a green gumtree
and a nectar-blackened hole in it
at which bees hovered and appeared —

Still unfocussed from the dream-prolonging
shower, this man sops lather,
stipples his face, then grades off
the Santa-wool of his shave
with flicks and whittlings.

Despite back yard and front garden
his children watch breakfast television
like Japanese in a miniature apartment
on the fiftieth floor. They
don't know a bywash from a bore-drain.

Splashed cologne won't sting the thought away.
It bothers him, knotting the tie
that will serve him for a beard
expounding lines in the boardroom:
his children don't come from his country.

Fatal, that in his own childhood
he walked up mortised stays
to the tops of strainer posts
on the coast of a wheat ocean.
It seeded in him the Narrabri reservation

with which he'll hear every scheme put forward today
Also by midday, when downtown wears the aspect
of towering sets left over from a nighttime
private-eye series, he'll recall how at midnight
the same buildings appear left over from the day

and will feel toward them the Narrabri reservation.
Not being the only person in his family
he won't start reading the Farm and Station ads
but will listen to the irony colleagues bring
to items in the paper: Ted's is the Katanning,

Laurel's will be the Gayndah reservation —
On the worn brakes of the city
all these instants of light friction.

The Up-to-date Scarecrow
for Melissa Gordon

With my mouldy felt hat and my coat pinned shut
I'd soon frighten nothing; birds'd sit on me — but
with some builders' plastic sheeting and a Coles bag on my
    head
I can dance standing still in a garden bed.
Ah, raggy plastic sheets! They're my favourite fad!
the best new idea the gardeners have had
for an old scarecrow (we scarecrows are born old):
they give me a voice, and the birds get told!
In any sort of breeze, in my polythene clothes
I can make crows vanish and men swear oaths —
fair crack of the whip! — when I put an elastic
snap to the air with a crinkle of my plastic,
and give me a wind blowing as wind can
I can crackle like eggs in a giant's frying pan!

The Cows on Killing Day

All me are standing on feed. The sky is shining.

All me have just been milked. Teats all tingling still
from that dry toothless sucking by the chilly mouths
that gasp loudly in in in, and never breathe out.

All me standing on feed, move the feed inside me.
One me smells of needing the bull, that heavy urgent me,
the back-climber, who leaves me humped, straining, but light
and peaceful again, with crystalline moving inside me.

Standing on wet rock, being milked, assuages the calf-sorrow
    in me.
Now the me who needs mounts on me, hopping, to signal
    the bull.

The tractor comes trotting in its grumble; the heifer human
bounces on top of it, and cud comes with the tractor,
big rolls of tight dry feed: lucerne, clovers, buttercup, grass,
that's been bitten but never swallowed, yet is cud.
She walks up over the tractor and down it comes, roll on roll
and all me following, eating it, and dropping the good pats.

The heifer human smells of needing the bull human
and is angry. All me look nervously at her
as she chases the dog me dream of horning dead: our enemy
of the light loose tongue. Me'd jam him in his squeals.

Me, facing every way, spreading out over feed.

One me is still in the yard, the place skinned of feed.
Me, old and sore-boned, little milk in that me now,
licks at the wood. The oldest bull human is coming.

Me in the peed yard. A stick goes out from the human
and cracks, like the whip. Me shivers and falls down
with the terrible, the blood of me, coming out behind an ear.
Me, that other me, down and dreaming in the bare yard.

All me come running. It's like the Hot Part of the sky
that's hard to look at, this that now happens behind wood
in the raw yard. A shining leaf, like off the bitter gum tree
is with the human. It works in the neck of me
and the terrible floods out, swamped and frothy. All me
    make the Roar,
some leaping stiff-kneed, trying to horn that worst horror.
The wolf-at-the-calves is the bull human. Horn the bull
    human!

But the dog and the heifer human drive away all me.

Looking back, the glistening leaf is still moving.
All of dry old me is crumpled, like the hills of feed,
and a slick me like a huge calf is coming out of me.

The carrion-stinking dog, who is calf of human and wolf,
is chasing and eating little blood things the humans scatter
and all me run away, over smells, toward the sky.

The Pole Barns

Unchinked log cabins, empty now, or stuffed with hay
under later iron. Or else roofless, bare stanzas of timber
with chars in the text. Each line ends in memorial
    axemanship.

With a hatch in one gable end, like a cuckoo clock,
they had to be climbed up into, or swung into
from the saddle of a quiet horse, feet-first onto corn.

On logs like rollers these rooms stand on creek flat and ridge,
and their true roofs were bark, every squared sheet a
    darkened
huge stroke of painting, fibrous from the brush.

Flattened, the sheets strained for a long time to curl again:
the man who slept on one and woke immobilised
in a scroll pipe is a primal pole-barn story.

The sound of rain on bark roofing, dotted, not pointed,
increasing to a sonic blanket, is millennia older than walls
but it was still a heart of storytelling, under the one lantern

as the comets of corn were stripped to their white teeth
and chucked over the partition, and the vellum husks
    shuffled down
round spooky tellers hunched in the planes of winter wind.

More a daylight thinker was the settler who noticed the tide
of his grain going out too fast, and set a dingo trap
in the servery slot — and found his white-faced neighbour,

a man bearded as himself, up to the shoulder in anguish.
Neither spoke as the trap was released, nor mentioned that
    dawn ever.
Happiest, in that iron age, were sitting aloft on the transom

unscrewing corn from cobs, making a good shower for the
    hens
and sailing the barn, with its log ram jutting low in front.
Like all the ships of conquest, its name was Supply.

The 1812 Overture at Topkapi Saray

The Rosary in Turkish, and prayers for the Sultān.
Through the filigree perforations of a curtain wall
a vagrant breeze parts a hanging mist of muslin
behind the Dowager Wife seated in her pavilion.

For fourteen hundred Sundays she has commended
to the Virgin's Son a fluctuating small congregation
of those who, like herself, had no choice about virginity:
concubines and eunuchs with the faces of aged children.

For perhaps thirteen hundred she has prayed for the Sultan,
both him to whom she was sent as a captured pearl
by the Bey of Algiers, and their son who reigns now in
      succession
beneath the inscriptions which, though she reads them
      fluently, still

at moments resemble tongues involved with a pastille,
or two, or three. The bitterest to her own taste
was never to succeed in stopping the trade in eunuchs
whereby little boys, never Muslim on the cutting day,

must be seated crying in hot, blood-stanching sand.
A sorrowful mystery. The traffic in bed-girls is another,
but there were eventually also joyous days
when the sea of Martinique yielded to the Marmara's glitter.

Now a messenger approaches the Executioner's House
beyond which only one entire man may pass
into this precinct on the headland of the city,
this Altai meadow of trees and marble tents.

An indifferent face is summoned to the grille
and the letter the messenger brings goes speeding on

31

to the woman concluding Glory Be among the cushions.
The rest withdraw, rustling, as she reads the superscription:

From the Commander of the Faithful to the Most Illustrious
Lady of the Seraglio — Mother, I have today
made a treaty with the Tsar, ceding one province
and retaining two we had also certainly lost.

These favourable terms arise from the Tsar's great need
of his army to face an invasion by the man Bonaparte,
Commander of the Faithless, to borrow your title for him.
Prospects for the Empire are improved at last

by this invasion, which will come. Russia is very great
but Bonaparte may defeat her. He may be Chinghiz Khan.
Our mightiest enemy would thereby be nullified
and such a victory might well ensnare the victor.

On the other hand, Bonaparte may lose — and then I think
with his legend broken, all Europe would turn on him
with Russia in the van, and engaged in that direction.
I must add, mother, that as I released the Tsar

for this coming contest, I had in mind our cousin
the Empress Josephine, dear playmate of your childhood
whom the Viper of the Nile so shamefully cast off
two years ago, in his quest for a Habsburg connection.

I was holding an exact balance: the choice was mine
to release the Tsar, or keep him engaged a while longer —
our treacherous Janissaries beat their spoons for this option.
If I held him, destruction of our old foe was assured:

I savoured that a little. Then I savoured his shielding us from
the spirit that drives France. As you taught me, the spirit is
    inseparable —
thus the honour of two wronged ladies tipped my decision.
Such moments, not I, are the shadow of God upon Earth. —

Aimée Dubucq de Rivéry, mother of the Sultan
walks in her pavilion, her son's letter trailing in her hand
and the carpets are a beach far beyond the Barbary pirates.
There she skips with Marie-Josèphe, her poor first cousin

but *poor* concerns parents only. A black manservant
attends each girl, as they splash filigree in the tide-edge
and gather it, as coral and pierced shells, which the men
    receive
for in that age young women are free, and men are passive.

From the Other Hemisphere

To stoop and insert
one leg between
the wires of a fence
and straighten with two
on the other side
is a way to enter
the Knack Museum,
as most will do.

Some there board trees,
some dry stone wall,
some can carry water
in an egg;
some there can stook
and some can full
and others bind puttees
tight on each leg.

With pensive butt in mouth
some can cut jacks and aces
or start a Model T
or make a bodice fit;
others can unzip a
live snake from its skin
or walk a biplane's wing
and think nothing of it.

Knacks old and new
and timeless too:
rulers who can daily
lie in state. —
That mystery you touched in
a skid, and lived
conjures worlds through the gap
between theory and sleight.

Stack coins edge on, or
as a sole toddler, poise
trembling-steady crystal goblets
stanza above stanza,
there's no morals in it:
you can turn from hanging farm-wives
to bust heroic bottles on
Panzer after Panzer.

A knack is embodied singing
in the brain's right wing:
to twirl a frail fire
out of a stick
gives measure to warm breath
from the first snow evening
and human history
reignites from the trick.

It's only the left mind
says before you die
you and all you love
will be obsolete —
our right mind, that shaped
this poem, paper, type-face,
has powerful if wordless
arguments against it.

Glaze

Tiles are mostly abstract:
tiles come from Islam:
tiles have been through fire:
tiles are a sacred charm:

After the unbearable parallel
trajectories of lit blank tile,
figure-tiles restore the plural,
figuring resumes its true vein.

Harm fades from the spirit as tiles
repeat time beyond time their riddle,
neat stanzas that rhyme from the middle
styles with florets with tendrils of balm.

Henna and mulberry mos-
aics controvert space:
lattice on lattice recedes
through itself into Paradise

or parrot starbursts framing themes
of stars bursting, until they salaam
the Holy Name in sprigged consonants
crosslaced as Welsh metrical schemes.

Conjunct, the infinite doorways
of the mansions of mansions amaze
underfoot in a cool court, with sun-blaze
afloat on the hard water of glaze.

Ur shapes under old liquor
ziggurats of endless incline;
cruciform on maiolica
flourishes the true vine.

Tulip tiles on the grate of Humoresque
Villa join, by a great arabesque
cream boudoirs of Vienna, then by left-
handed rhyme, the blue pubs of Delft

and prominence stands in a circle
falling to the centre of climb:
O miming is defeated by mime:
circles circle the PR of ominence.

Cool Mesach in fused Rorschach,
old from beyond Islam,
tiles have been to Paradise,
clinkers of ghostly calm.

Farmer at Fifty

He could envisage
though he didn't invent
the breeze-steered dam
in its khaki pug,
cattle twinned at their drinking
and the baby frogs
still in their phlegm.

Woodducks drowsing on their feet
enriching the dam wall,
he could foresee them,
but not the many jets
of the native waterlily
burning Bunsen-blue
on many a high stem

out of leaf-clouds
on the anchored stream.
He didn't know they'd come.
But: what he'd done, stopping
erosive water's hurry
had also been to build
a room for them.

The same with home.
He could foresee
daily bunting on the line,
white, pink, swallowtail and square
flags announcing a baby
but not what came then,
nor who had come;

not what childhoods he'd be in
and left in, eventually.
On the dam wall, the dog
sits beside its tail
and turns its head with him
as he looks into the tops
of the trees downstream.

The Tube
for Ann Moyal and Rob Crawford

Many resemble Henry Sutton
in sleevelinks in Ballarat
who invented television;
later several would do that
but not in eighteen eighty seven.

"Telephany" — he named it well:
his Greek was more correct.
His design was theoretical
but: Nipkow disc and Kerr effect
and selenium photocell,

all were there. It would have worked
and brought the Melbourne Cup alive
to Ballarat, which was his object —
but no one had yet sent an aerial wave
and wire had this defect:

signals couldn't race so fast
along it that they'd sustain a picture.
Only when the horse-drawn age was past
could horses surge into the air
with music and gunfire, galloping broadcast.

Tremendous means, and paltry vision:
some will dare ask you about that
in your interview, Henry Sutton,
in Ballarat, in your floreat,
standing telephanous on your front lawn.

Shale Country

Watermelon rinds around the house,
small gondolas of curling green
lined with sodden rosy plush;
concrete paths edged with kerosene,

tricycles and shovels in the yard
where the septic tank makes a fairy ring;
a wire gate leads into standing wheat,
cream weatherboard overlaps everything —

and on the wheatless side, storm-blue
plaques curl off the spotted-gum trees
which, in new mayonnaise trunks, stand over
a wheelbarrow on its hands and knees.

Barrenjoey

Along Sydney's upraised finger
diced suburbs mass and hide
in bush, or under brilliant towels
that swirl — or brace and glide
man-hung out over blue horizons
that roll in on the land.
Twinned dips, with imprinted nipples
or not, cool in the sand,
and castles top odd headlands
and rarely a shark-bell rings;
loud-hailers honk French: Cardin! Croissants!
and detectives wear G-strings.

Where the poet Brennan wandered
the soaked steeps of his mind
now men and women warily
strike deals that can't be signed.
Where once in salt sheet-iron days
a girl might halt her filly
under posies atop cornstalks three yards high,
groves of the Gymea lily,
the northward sandstone finger, knobbed
with storms and strange injections
has beckoned Style, and Porsche windscreens
glimmer with cool deflections —

but Pittwater's still a quiver of masts
and Broken Bay in the sun
is seamed with tacking arrowheads
and that's always gone on.
Modest wealth's made a paradise garden
of that range and its green sound
so to throw sand in the evil eye
some scandal must be found.
To flesh a bone for envy's pup
now scandals must be found.

The International Terminal

Some comb oil, some blow air,
some shave trenchlines in their hair
but the common joint thump, the heart's spondee
kicks off in its rose-lit inner sea
like an echo, at first, of the one above
it on the dodgy ladder of love —
and my mate who's driving says *I never*
found one yet worth staying with forever.
In this our poems do not align.
Surely most are if you are, answers mine,
and I am living proof of it,
I gloom, missing you from the cornering outset —
and hearts beat mostly as if they weren't there,
rocking horse to rocking chair,
most audible dubbed on the tracks of movies
or as we approach where our special groove is
or our special fear. The autumn-vast
parking-lot-bitumen overcast
now switches on pumpkin-flower lights
all over dark green garden sites
and a wall of car-bodies, stacked by blokes,
obscures suburban signs and smokes.
Like coughs, cries, all such unlearned effects
the heartbeat has no dialects
but what this or anything may mean
depends on what poem we're living in.
Now a jet engine, huge child of a gun,
shudders with haze and begins to run.
Over Mount Fuji and the North Pole
I'm bound for Europe in a reading role
and a poem long ago that was coming for me
had Fuji-san as its axle-tree.
Cities shower and rattle over the gates
as I enter that limbo between states
but I think of the heart swarmed round by poems

like an egg besieged by chromosomes
and how out of that our world is bred
through the back of a mirror, with clouds in its head
— and airborne, with a bang, this five-hundred-seat
theatre folds up its ponderous feet.

Granite Country

Out above the level
in enormous room
beyond the diagram fences
eggs of the granite loom.

In droughts' midday hum,
at the crack of winter,
horizons of the tableland
are hatched out of them

and that levelling forces
all the more to rise
past swamp, or thumbwhorled ploughing,
tor, shellback, cranium

in unended cold eruption.
Forces and strains of granite
ascended from a kingdom
abandon over centuries

their craft on the sky-rim,
sprung and lichened hatches,
as, through gaps in silence, what
made itself granite goes home.

The Ocean Baths

Chinning the bar or Thirties concrete rim
of this ocean baths as the surf flings velleities of spray
brimming the bright screen
I am in not the sea but the sea's television.

As the one starfish below me quivers up
through a fictive kelp of diffraction, I'm thinking of workers
who made pool-cementing last, neap tide by neap,
right through the Depression

then went to the war, the one that fathered the Bomb
which relegated war to the lurid antique new nations
of emerging television. All those appalling horizontals
to be made vertical and kept the size of a screen —

I duck out of focus
down chill slub walls in this loud kinking room
that still echoes *Fung blunger* the swearwords *Orh you*
    Kongs
of men on relief for years, trapping ocean in oblongs,

and check out four hard roads tamed to a numinous
joke on it all, through being stood up side-on
and joined at their stone ends by bumper-smokers who
    could,
just by looking up, see out of relegation —

here the sky, the size of a mirror, the size of a fix
becomes imperative: I explode up through it beneath
a whole flowering height of villas and chlorine tiled pools
where some men still swear hard
to keep faith with their fathers the poor, obsolete and sacred.

Three Last Stanzas

That's the choice: most
as failures and tools
or an untrustworthy host
of immortal souls.

O

The owl who eats living
mice in the gloom
is still in the long
rehearsals for your freedom.

O

Absolutely anything
is absolute to those
who see the poem in it.
Relegation is prose.

Mirror-glass Skyscrapers

After cruelly yanked palazzi,
steel bridges stood on end in air,
flak-tower and liftwell skeletons
middlebrow with glazing, at last
postliteral architecture is here:

jade suits pitched frameless up the sky
drift all day with sheer weather,
annexed cubes ascend and blend
at chisel points away high
on talc-green scintillant towers,

diurnal float glass apparitions:
through their aspects airliners flow,
their decoration's anything that happens.
Even their height above suburb
is reflected. Perfect borrowers' rococo!

Outside, squared, has finally gone in,
closed over like steadying water,
to quote storms, to entertain strapped gondolas
and loose giants swimming in contour.
Inside yearning out isn't seen;

work's turned its back on sweat brilliantly —
but when they start to loom, these towers
disappear. Dusk's lightswitches reveal
yellow Business branching kilotall
and haloed with stellar geometry.

The Lieutenant of Horse Artillery

Full tilt for my Emperor and King, I
galloped down the moonlit roads of Hungary
past poplar after Lombardy poplar tree
in our dear multicultural Empi-

re alas! on a horse I didn't know
had been requisitioned from a circus. Without fail
he leaped every tree-shadow lying like a fox's tail
over the road, O despite whip, despite Whoa!

unswerving, he hurdled them. My leather shako jerked,
my holster slapped my hip, my despatch case too,
every leap! I was clubbed black and blue
inside my tight trousers. So many shadows lurked

to make him soar and me cry out, taking wing
every fifty metres the length of a desperate ride
for my Emperor and King, as our Empire died
with its dream of happy cultures dancing in a ring.

Dog Fox Field

The test for feeblemindedness was, they had to make up a
sentence using the words dog, fox *and* field.

Judgement at Nuremberg

These were no leaders, but they were first
into the dark on Dog Fox Field:

Anna who rocked her head, and Paul
who grew big and yet giggled small,

Irma who looked Chinese, and Hans
who knew his world as a fox knows a field.

Hunted with needles, exposed, unfed,
this time in their thousands they bore sad cuts

for having gazed, and shuffled, and failed
to field the lore of prey and hound

they then had to thump and cry in the vans
that ran while stopped in Dog Fox Field.

Our sentries, whose holocaust does not end,
they show us when we cross into Dog Fox Field.

Hastings River Cruise

i.m. Ruth and Harry Liston, d. Port Macquarie 1826

Getting under way in that friendly suburb of balconies
we were invited to imagine up to thirty woollen ships
and timber ships and beef ships with fattening sails
along the one-time quay. Then down Heaven-blued
olive water of the estuary, we saw how ocean's crystal
penned up riverine tinctures. On our coast, every river
is a lake, for lack of force, and lives within its colour bar.

Upstream, past the bullock-faced and windjammer-ballasted
   shore
we passed where men in canary flannel were worked
   barefoot
on oystershells in shark tides. No one's walked in Australia
since, for pride and sympathy. Sheds lay offshore, pegged to
   the water
and lascivious oysters, though they are nearly all tongue
didn't talk drink, on their racks of phlegm, but lived it.
Opposite lay the acre where Queensland was first planted

as the pineapple of cropped heads in hot need of sugar walls.
There too, by that defiance, were speedboat mansions up
   canals
and no prescriptive ulcers or divorces apparent in them
though one, built late in life perhaps, spilled grapefruit down
   its lawns.
And the river curved on, and a navy-backed elephant stood
in the mountains for mission boys who stepped right up,
   through the drum,
and belted blue eyes into red-leather Kingdom Come.

At the highway bridge, in sight of plateaux, we turned back
and since the shore of the present was revetments and raw
   brick

or else flood-toppled trees with mullet for foliage, I looked
over at the shore of the past. Rusty paddocks, with out-of-
    date palms,
punt ramps where De Sotos crossed; there, in houses patched
    with tan,
breezeways wound to green bedrooms with framed words
    like He Moaneth,
the sort of country I might traverse during death.

Returning downstream, over the Regatta Ground's liquid
    tiling,
we passed through the place where, meeting his only sister
in a new draft to the Port, the tugged escapee snatched the
    musket
of a redcoat captor, aimed and shot her dead —
and was saluted for it, as he strangled, by the Commandant.
In sight of new motels, this opposite potential stayed defined
and made the current town look remote, and precarious, and
    kind.

Gun-e-Darr

The red serpent of cattle, that eclipsed the old dreaming
      serpents,
there it still is, the first stock route, winding out of far lilac
      ranges
onto the grassed sea-floor of the plain. The shortest distance
between two points being, in life, the serpentine,
it was dissimulation to have angled it to a crankshaft
of official roads. I see it now, smoking high and raw with dust
as it curved and lengthened in its first days. And if taking
the continent was no walkover, then there were brave men
on both sides, amid the bellowing, the scattering whipcrack
      undulations
and sleepy flooding onward of the blood-red cattle serpent,
destroyer of sacred dance circles, and equally of little hoed
      farms.

Words of the Glassblowers

In a tacky glass-foundry yard, that is shadowy and bright
as an old painter's sweater stiffening with light,

another lorry chockablock with bottles gets the raised thumb
and there hoists up a wave like flashbulbs feverish in a
    stadium

before all mass, nosedive and ditch, colour showering to grit,
starrily, mutually, becoming the crush called cullet

which is fired up again, by a thousand degrees, to a mucilage
and brings these reddened spearmen bantering on stage.

Each fishes up a blob, smoke-sallow with a tinge of beer
which begins, at a breath, to distill from weighty to clear

and, spinning, is inflated to a word: the paraison
to be marvered on iron, box-moulded, or whispered to while
    spun —

Sand, sauce-bottle, hourglass — we melt them into one thing:
that old Egyptian syrup, that tightens as we teach it to sing.

High Sugar

Honey gave sweetness
to Athens and Rome,
and later, when splendour
might rise nearer home,

sweetness was still honey
since, pious or lax,
every cloister had its apiary
for honey and wax

but when kings and new doctrines
drained those deep hives
then millions of people
were shipped from their lives

to grow the high sugar
from which were refined
frigates, perukes, human races
and the liberal mind.

Spotted Native Cat

He's done me, has that bastard Sanderson
that I sank dams for on his huge mountain run.
Eighteen months and damn near the wreck
of my business from the lies he spread — now I get his
    cheque
and it's pure rubber!
                    Hold on to it, says my wife,
who has this patient slant on life.
You know the legend of the spotted native cat
who shows his enemy Brown Snake the fat
possum he's just speared, gives it that to eat instead
then, as it lies sated, bites off its head
and devours them both? —
                    So I'm in the bank door
every Friday arv. The cheque's still Refer to Drawer
every time. For some weeks, the manager glowers
but finally he takes me for a drink after hours
and murmurs confidentially that Sanderson's account
is just three hundred shy of the cheque amount —
and my wife says You see?
                 So what's our next dart? —
We could raise that much ourselves, but where's the art
in that? — Or the vengeance? The punishment? — Dear
    heart!
Sanderson sells more cattle than he breeds,
they say, and has more children than he feeds —
But they're low angles, like going to the law,
which gets, and is reckoned as, a very low score
between men, in the bush —
               Between new and old debtors
too, eh? We being new here — Wait! Have we got letters
from his bank, with signature and letterhead? —
I think I can get such notepaper blank, she said,
and the school's electric typewriter. Ex-students are a
    blessing. —

Can a bodgie cheque be stopped? —
                              In three days, I get a pressing
invitation to come up to Sanderson's eyrie
but I don't care to fuel his anonymous theory
that I'm after his daughter, so I stipulate
that we meet at the Greek's in town. Tomorrow. Mate.
Or anyway check.
                    After only a short beat
around the bush, he comes to the meat
of the matter. He doesn't understand the banks'
new fussiness about cheque accounts. Bloody cranks!
But to save bad blood he'll buy my one back
for half its face value (I do not crack
a smile) and pay me the rest real soon
when he just gets his share from subletting the moon
(my attention wandered there). A light sweat
moistens his scalp and ringbarked haircut.
And I agree.
                    And to my amazement
he gives his mahogany tea an intent
suck, and begins to wheedle me down
to a quarter. I very nearly drown
in my suppressed laughter, but my face
nods in many mirrors with good grace,
and again I agree.
                    The possum is now fat,
spiced with just a whiff of rat.
He ha I don't spose you'll take a cheque? —
He ha I don't think so. — He deals from a deck
of fifties pallid from long damp storage.
Thanks. Now I'll clear the cheque for you. — Rage
slowly darkens the planed boards of his face:
You've got it at the bank then? —
                              It's in a safe place —
It almost rattles me, how instantly his gaze
assumes the tranced blue of drought-time days,
dismissing me. I wish he'd shout and heave
his chair through the cafe's cellophane treasures.
                              But I leave

and pay his money into his account
and cash our cheque for its full amount
and pay our fuel bills and save our hide
and realise I'm now on the mountain man's side.

Levities of the Short Giant

Afternoon, and the Short Giant takes his siesta
on a threadbare ruby sofa which, being shorter than he,
curves him into the half moon or slice-of-pawpaw position,
hull down, like a deep-timbered merchantman, with both
    hands on deck,
his stubbled head for poop and lantern, and at the bow
twin figureheads: bare feet with soles the earthen green
of seed potatoes, rimmed with old paintings' craquelure.
Massive mosquito-scabbed legs slope down into dungaree;
asleep in his own arms, he makes odd espresso noises.

This man, who warms cold ground by lying on it, who hand-
    parks his car,
who knows in his shoulders crab from scissors from flying
    mare
is most of all the man who attaches the thick wheels
and coins of weight, the bronzes and black steels,
and hoists (tingling) them, from knees to arrh! collarbone to
    full
extension overhead, the left and the right, bending his milled
    bar
— I breathe them up, shutting my thighs, and those fat ladies
    sing
to crack my spine's teeth. O but when I drop them, they ding
the stage hollow, jolt gravity itself, and chuck me in the air!

On Removing Spiderweb

Like summer silk its denier
but stickily, o ickilier,
miffed bunny-blinder, silver tar,
gesticuli-gesticular,
crepe when cobbed, crap when rubbed,
stretchily adhere-and-there
and everyway, nap-snarled or sleek,
glibly hubbed with grots to tweak:
ehh weakly bobbined tae yer neb,
spit it Phuoc Tuy! filthy web!

The Assimilation of Background

Driving on that wide jute-coloured country
we came at last to the station,
its homestead with lawn and steel awnings
like a fortress against the sun.
And when we knocked, no people answered;
only a black dog came politely
and accompanied us round the verandahs
as we peered into rooms, and called brightly
Anyone home? The billiard room,
shadowed dining room, gauze-tabled kitchen
gave no answer. Cricket bats, ancient
steamer trunks, the chugging coolroom engine
disregarded us. Only the dog's very patient
claws ticked with us out of the gloom
to the grounds' muffling dust, to the machine shed
black with oil and bolts, with the welder
mantis-like on its cylinder of clocks
and then to the stallion's enclosure.
The great bay horse came up to the wire,
gold flares shifting on his muscles, and stood
as one ungelded in a thousand
of his race, but imprisoned for his sex,
a gene-transmitting engine, looking at us
gravely as a spirit, out between
his brain's potent programmes. Then a heifer,
Durham-roan, but with Brahman hump and rings
around her eyes, came and stood among us
and a dressy goat in sable and brushed fawn
ogled us for offerings beyond
the news all had swiftly gathered from us
in silence, and could, it seemed, accept.
We had been received, and no one grew impatient
but only the dog, host-like, walked with us

back to our car. The lawn-watering sprays
ticked over, and over. And we saw
that out on that bare, crusted country
background and foreground had merged;
nothing that existed there was background.

Araucaria Bidwilli

Big leaves of the native tamarind,
vein-gathered, spread coppery black-green.

Finger-bone beads, refreshing, sour-sweet,
are the amber berries of the native tamarind.

Nearby to far up kink invisibly winging
calls, above vine-strung palisade tracks

and over steep gullies, on the ringing mountain:
stupendous, racial green, the first crosstreed soaring

allosaur-skinned primeval pines, their shrapnel
cones dizzying above gullies, on the rayed mould mountain,

lanterns of fitted flour, that can drop to kill
on once-sacred gullies, along the two-peaked mountain.

These are the trees that teach me again
every tradition is a choke on metaphor

yet the limits to likeness don't imprison its ends,
climbing above gullies, through mote-drift on the mountain.

Spring

A window glimmering in wheeltracked clay
and someone skipping on the windowsill;
spins of her skipping-rope widen away.
She is dancing light and water
out of the cold side of the hill
and I've brought rhyme to meet her;
rhyme has been ill.

The Import of Adult Flavours

Small birds flitting where twigs interleave
are innocent, but not naive.
Like unprotected humans, they
sing and flirt all on the qui vive.

When Europe sold scorn of innocence
it seemed to the old poor partly sense
but more a mere blackening of all green,
hard labour at will, without the sentence.

A soft-palm frisson, a gambit to snare
cold luxury nestled inside despair,
it formed a spy-mad police interlude between
self pity and hard drugs everywhere.

Accordion Music

A backstrapped family Bible that consoles virtue and sin,
for it opens top and bottom, and harps both out and in:

it shuffles a deep pack of cards, flirts an inverted fan
and stretches to a shelf of books about the pain of man.

It can play the sob in Jesus!, the cavernous *baastards* note,
it can wheedle you for cigarettes or drop a breathy quote:

it can conjure Paris up, or home, unclench a chinstrap jaw
but it never sang for a nob's baton, or lured the boys to war.

Underneath the lone streetlight outside a crossroads hall
where bullocks pass and dead girls waltz and mental
     gum trees fall

two brothers play their plough-rein days and long gone
     spoon-licked nights.
The fiddle stitching through this quilt lifts up in singing
     flights,

the other's mourning, meaning tune goes arching up and
     down
as life undulates like a heavy snake through the rocked
     accordion.

Experiential

Rubbish! As the twig is bent the tree does not grow, at all.
In fact, on the high side of the bend small new twigs appear
and the strongest becomes a new trunk, and restores the
vertical.

The Greenhouse Vanity

Sea-perch over paddocks. Dunes. Salt light everywhere low
    down
just like the increasing gleam between Bass Strait hills
nine thousand years ago. In an offshore crumbling town
the Folk Museum moans of a stormy night, and shrills:

You made the oceans rise! Nonsense, it was you!
The Pioneers Room and Recent Times are quarrelling.
By day the flannelled drone: up at daylight, lard and tea,
axe and crosscut till black dark, once I shot a ding-

o at the cradle, there at fifteen, the only white woman
ploughing by hand, parrot pie, we sewed our own music —
Recent Times blink and hum; one bends to B-cup a pair,
each point the rouge inside a kiss; one boosts the tape-deck:

Hey launder your earnings with a Green gig: show you care!
Rock millionaire,
When every city's Venice we'll all go to Venus, yeah!
Smoke green shit there

— till coal conveyors rattle and mile-high smokestacks pant
Beige! beige! on every viewscreen. This should re-float your
    Hardships,
despoiler, black-shooter! — Nature's caught up with you,
    Trendywank! —
So. We changed the weather. — Yep. Humans. We made and
    unmade the maps.

An Australian History of the Practical Man

This is the man
who took over from evolution,

the unbearable servant
who gives us what we want.

Our peace is the foam
on his current, our reality
a stage in practicality.

If our wars are our own
it is through him we win.

He's not the composer in steels
whose sonatas have wheels
or wear chains to fly a firth. That's his twin.

But have a moral dream —
and ships and the knotted lash are one more solution
he comes up with for you,

ships for vanishment, triangle
to secure both floggee and clear view.
Cheerful terrible being,

he enacts every logic you can't face —
and the land's cleared for settlement
with arsenic and gun.

Disown him. He would you.
Make him a dusty clown
with his portable soup, his wire rope and bush chutney:

that's plum jam mixed with Worcester sauce . . .
then suddenly your life's given back
by his needle in your heart, his electric force.

He conjures up water and grass
with a piped spear, flies doctors, wires horses,

then, as you wished, he's
delivered your sour attrition
of land-bought leisure, made you your sex machine

and gone aloft on your terror of him. Gone.
Look for him in the cities of Yen
and at the farthest spring-clip out in space,

a beckon or hook of metal on a line
unfalling there in space.

Slip

This week, one third of Australia is under water.
— Sydney newspaper report, 9 April 1989

Over the terra cotta
speeds a mirrored sun
on bare and bush-mossed water
as a helicopter's stutter
signals a stock-feed run,

and cubic fodder-bombs splash
open on sodden islands.
In their yolk of orange squash,
tugging out each mud galosh,
sheep climb those twenty-inch highlands,

and vehicles at a miles-wide rushing
break in the human map
stare mesmerised at the whooshing
pencil strokes that kink where a crushing
car rolls, and turns on like a tap.

A realised mirage reaches
into tack-sheds and yards
and laps undreamed-of beaches
wadded with shock-tranced creatures.
Millennia of red-walled clouds

have left the creekbeds unable
to let the spreading glaze
spill off the water table,
though here and there a cable
braids light between crumbling cays.

Hand-milling tobacco, each dent
in his bronze oilskin adrip,
the scraped owner surveys the extent
of death-slog when the red-ware continent
glistens next week in its slip,

and when all the shapes and shallows
of inland ocean turn grass
and scarlets and purples and yellows,
when lizards eat clouds in jammed hollows
and horizons turn back into glass.

Aircraft Stressed-skin Blowout
Mid-Pacific

(United Airlines Flight 811)

The miles-high bubble civility
ruptured, and instantly the tear
stormed with a jetlike volatility
of baggage shoes people into air
darkly white and shrilling as the pole
that every unbuckled thing was whirling to.
Windmilling toward seats already nowhere
a member of the cabin crew
was going with the West out the hole
when legs in a scissor lock around her
and male hands in her clothes before the blue
absolute mastered it, raped her of fall
then, under restored equal pressure,
gestured in a tear-halo with joking humility.

In Murray's Dictionary

The word *aplace*
lasted from Gower to the Puritans
but never got much use,
yet far from being obscure, it once
was more of a true antonym
to *away* than say *back* or *home*,
here, *present* or *fixed in space*:
"The king's away, but I'm aplace
and shan't abandon him."

Aplace was maybe an embrace
too fixed and metaphysical
for the Anglophone genius,
somewhere lost, fled from or paradisiacal
where we'd know, or knew, our place.
Germans have no such fear:
da means both *there* and *here*,
but perhaps we sailed away
in our prize ship the Renaissance,

ravaging the locative case,
even voiding revolution that way,
shipping it out of every county
to erupt on Boston and the Bounty,
venturing impatiently apace
till locality was nowhere
and only God was there,
invisible, in the lay sense,
the Darwinian modern-day sense

that grows from a youthful enmity,
and it would take extremity
to make us reappear.

Ariel

Upward, cheeping, on huddling wings,
these small brown mynas have gained
a keener height than their kind ever sustained
but whichever of them fails first
falls to the hawk circling under
who drove them up.
Nothing's free when it is explained.

Politics and Art

Brutal policy,
like inferior art, knows
whose fault it all is.

Major Sparrfelt's Trajectory

Öland, Southern Baltic, 1 June 1676

Our ship was a rope-towered town
built inside its own wall;
carved Romans, niches, mantlings in gilt
made its stern a palace, a Popish cathedral.

That day as we joined battle
my sword swung so wide with the tilt
our mighty *Crown* assumed, turning
that my crossed right hand missed its hilt

as from lidded and horsecollar ports
the ponderous ship's cannon ran back:
shrieks mingled with bronze thunder below
— all life then split upward with the crack

of glare that stripped my rational mind
and left me in the one mind of animals.
I flew above crosstrees, over lightning-defined
tangling and clubbed recoil of ships,

every cannon-hit a tube of mortal screams
burrowed deep in a closing gun-wall;
soldiers' massed steel heads bent to muskets
thick as cart-shafts, which squirted a blue pall.

Swordsmen, blood-seekers, crisscrossed everywhere,
letting some from one, from another all,
blood of men, as of fowls and beasts; these *pompiers
funèbres* in their leaping Aztec skill

were true limbs of perpetual motion.
Remembrance never touched me, overhead,
angel to fragments, that I too was such a one.
Removed, I watched as from the dead,

orbiting the royal park of mastheads
like a soul through war's updraft of souls,
above where men flared flintlocks intently,
flung, plunged, hung seeping in cloth scrolls

above a chipped sea of continual white tussocks,
of drifting fires, collapsed floats, drinking men,
Swedish blue, Danish red — a cloud-wide bolster
of foresail canvas caught me then

and I slid, grabbed, tumbled to the deck
of our own king's frigate *Draken*.
By a singular grace of the Almighty
lifted out of death by the rays of detonation,

I lived fifty-four more years, fought the Tsar,
saw great-grandchildren, was Münchhausen's uncle,
    governed Gotland,
but never attained the disembodying era
of television, that I'd foreshadowed. Yet in my life of
    command

a similar vantage of death would never leave me.
Red health and fierce moustaches
still served their turn, and were true
in the world of acts, but no longer could deceive me;

as a smiling woman said once: Colonel, you
I imagine saying *I'll miss me when I'm gone*.
I partly have, but there's true foretaste and gain
in those times even fear's tight wig will not stay on.

A Torturer's Apprenticeship

Those years trapped in a middling cream town
where full-grown children hold clear views
and can tell from his neck he's really barefoot
though each day he endures shoes,

he's what their parents escaped, the legend
of dogchained babies on Starve Gut Creek;
be friends with him and you will never
be shaved or uplifted, cool or chic.

He blusters shyly — poverty can't afford instincts.
Nothing protects him, and no one.
He must be suppressed, for modernity,
for youth, for speed, for sexual fun.

Also, believing as tacitly as he
that only dim Godly joys are equal
while the competitive, the exclusive
class pleasures are imperative evil

they see him as a nascent devil,
wings festering to life in his weekly shirt,
and daily go for the fist-and-finger
hung at the arch of keenest hurt.

Slim revenge of sorority. He must shoot birds,
discard the love myth and search for clues.
But for the blood-starred barefoot spoor
he found, this one might have made dark news.

The Ballad of the Barbed Wire Ocean

No more rice pudding. Pink coupons for Plume. Smokes
    under the lap for aunts.
Four running black boots beside a red sun. Flash wireless
    words like Advarnce.
When the ocean was wrapped in barbed wire, terror radiant
    up the night sky,
exhilaration raced flat out in squadrons; Mum's friends took
    off sun-hats to cry.

Starting south of the then world with new showground rifles
    being screamed at and shown
for a giggle-suit three feeds a day and no more plans of your
    own,
it went with some swagger till God bless you, Tom! and
    Daddy come back! at the train
or a hoot up the gangways for all the girls and soon the coast
    fading in rain,

but then it was flared screams from blood-bundles whipped
    rolling as iron bombs keened down
and the insect-eyed bombers burned their crews alive in off-
    register henna and brown.
In steep ruins of rainforest pre-affluent thousands ape-
    scuttling mixed sewage with blood
and fear and the poem played vodka to morals, fear jolting to
    the mouth like cud.

It was sleep atop supplies, it was pickhandle, it was coming
    against the wall in tears,
sometimes it was factory banter, stoking jerked breechblocks
    and filing souvenirs,
or miles-wide humming cattleyards of humans, or oiled ship-
    fires slanting in ice,
rag-wearers burst as by huge War Bonds coins, girls' mouths
    full of living rice.

No one came home from it. Phantoms smoked two hundred
    daily. Ghosts held civilians at bay,
since war turns beyond strut and adventure to keeping what
    you've learned, and shown,
what you've approved, and what you've done, from ever
    reaching your own.
This is died for. And nihil and nonsense feed on it day after
    day.

Midnight Lake

Little boy blue, four hours till dawn.
Your bed's a cement bag, your plastic is torn.

Your breakfast was tap water, dinner was sleep;
you are the faith your olds couldn't keep.

In your bunny rug room there were toys on the floor
but nothing is obvious when people get poor

and newspaper crackles next to your skin.
You're a newspaper fairytale now, Tommy Thin,

a postnatal abortion, slick outer space thing,
you run like a pinball BING! smack crack BING!

then, strung out and spotty, you wriggle and sigh
and kiss all the fellows and make them all die.

Spitfire Roundel

Nothing like a cool experiment in strict form
to tap the hurt fury that distils in us like an element
to react with our self-control and blaze and storm,
    nothing like a cool experiment.

The form is then arch jokes, implying our real Main Event
is remote, yet in the bag, keeping our old money warm.
About the odd spill en route we must be intelligent

and let the unruffled style brick us up in a snob-school dorm
despite our real pain — and damn the inverted
    compliment —
and our passion being well up to the first-love norm,
    nothing like a cool experiment.

Antarctica

Beyond the human flat earths
which, policed by warm language, wreathe
in fog the limits of the world,
far out in space you can breathe

the planet revolves in a cold book.
It turns one numb white page a year.
Round this in shattering billions spread
ruins of a Ptolemaic sphere,

and brittle-beard reciters bore
out time in adamant hoar rods
to freight where it's growing short,
childless absolutes shrieking the odds.

Most modern of the Great South Lands,
her storm-blown powder whited wigs
as wit of the New Contempt chilled her.
The first spacefarers worked her rope rigs

in horizontal liftoff, when to climb
the high Pole was officer class.
Total prehuman pavement, extending
beyond every roof-brink of crevasse:

Sterility Park, ringed by sheathed animals.
Singing spiritoso their tongueless keens
musselled carollers fly under the world.
Deeper out, our star's gale folds and greens.

Blue miles above the first flowered hills
towers the true Flood, as it was,
as it is, at the crux of global lattice,
and long-shod humans, risking diamond, steam
propitiating it with known laws and our wickedness.

Distinguo

Prose is Protestant-agnostic,
story, discussion, significance,
but poetry is Catholic:
poetry is presence.

The Past Ever Present

Love is always an awarded thing
but some are no winners, of no awarding class.
Each is a song that they themselves can't sing.

For months of sundays, singlehanded under iron, with the
    flies,
they used to be safe from that dizzying small-town sex
whose ridicule brought a shamed evasion to their eyes.

Disdaining the relegated as themselves, they eyed the
    vividest
for whom inept gentleness without prestige was *slow*.
Pity even the best, then, when they're made second best.

Consider the self-sentenced who heel the earth round with
    shy feet
and the wallflower who weeps not from her eyes but her
    palms
and those who don't master the patter, or whom the codes
    defeat.

If love is always an awarded thing
some have cursed the judging and screamed off down old
    roads
and all that they killed were the song they couldn't sing.

Like the Joy at His First Lie

Paradises of limitation, charm
of perpetual doughy innocence —
how quickly the reality
scrubs such stuff from mind.
Today, at eleven and a half,
he made his first purchase:
forty cents, for two biscuits, no change
but a giant step into mankind.

The House of Worth

Mirror, mirror, on the whole
you've been a bastard to my soul
and more believe mirrors than self esteem
and belief's halfway to dream
    The iced tea a winter sunrise pours
    through regrowth forest has its flaws
    and serious minds know what they are
    but like the triskel Mercedes star
    a cat in repose has a three-cornered mouth
    and if trees are dying, and not of drouth,
    voilà the toxin in each one's phloem:
    the Enlightenment's a Luciferian poem
O knowledge hangs from a speed in space
but it tells a good tale, if it keeps off race
and for all of England's mews and hedges
and Holland's stormy upturned edges
and those death's head caps collecting fares
across cobblestones like toffee squares,
not Europe, you can tell the birds and bees,
but Atlantis is Australia's antipodes
    To make a likeness entirely true
    is more than truth itself can do,
    this was so that you might be free
    and why the bread is fully gone
    in what has no comparison.
    Likewise what's drunk can afford to be,
    while the hay is golden as the calf
    or the mountain, and no one's a better half
    for surely, when equality is complete
    there can be no mortal thing to eat
And I am of the house of Worth:
it was my grandmother's name at birth
and images, we know, are as limb to leg
so who is chicken? What is egg?

Blue Roan

for Philip Hodgins

As usual up the Giro mountain
dozers were shifting the road about
but the big blue ranges looked permanent
and the stinging-trees held no hint of drought.

All the high drill and blanket ridges
were dusty for want of winter rains
but down in the creases of picnic oak
brown water moved like handled chains.

Steak-red Herefords, edged like steaks
with that creamy fat the health trade bars
nudged, feeding, settling who'd get horned
and who'd horn, in the Wingham abattoirs

and men who remembered droughttime grass
like three days' growth on a stark red face
described farms on the creeks, fruit trees and fun
and how they bought out each little place.

Where farm families once would come just to watch
men knock off work, on the Bulliac line,
the fear of helplessness still burned live brush.
Dirty white smoke sent up its scattered sign

and in at the races and out at home
the pump of morale was primed and bled:
"Poor Harry in the street, beer running out his eyes,"
as the cousin who married the baker said.

The Road Toll

for those most recently slaughtered on the roads

Toll. You are part of the toll
government causes, and harps on, and exacts
as more toll. The word means both death and taxes.

Trains are government, so they don't pay, toll. Trucks pay
and pay, and pay. Speed narrows the wrecked highway
as fines, based on the death toll, are increased continually.

So you justify, and your stretchers drip, the toll
we must pay for the juggernaut Government,
for every Crown careerist's inner greasy pole,
for the logic of swift movement —

It's crocodile tears, toll, except from those who loved you.
Your death taps us for revenue. You were driving on the
     railway
and we'll all be fined for it. You were a tin boat on the sea
and a ship ran over you. A fleeing merchantman, toll.

An Era

The poor were fat and the rich were lean.
Nearly all could preach, very few could sing.
The fashionable were all one age, and to them
a church picnic was the very worst thing.

The Gaelic Long Tunes

On Sabbath days, on circuit days,
the Free Church assembled from boats and gigs
and between sermons they would tauten
and, exercising all they allowed of art,
haul on the long lines of the Psalms.

The seated precentor, touching text,
would start alone, lifting up his whale-long tune
and at the right quaver, the rest set sail
after him, swaying, through eerie and lorn.
No unison of breaths-in gapped their sound.

In disdain of all theatrics, they raised
straight ahead, from plank rows, their beatless God-paean,
their giving like enduring. And in rise
and undulation, in Earth-conquest mourned
as loss, all tragedy drowned, and that weird
music impelled them, singing, like solar wind.

Wagtail

Willy Wagtail
sings at night
black and white
Oz nightingale
   picks spiders off wall
   nest-fur and eyesocket
   ticks off cows
   cattle love that
Busy daylong
eating small species
makes little faeces
and a great wealth of song
   Will and Willa Wagtail
   indistinguishable
   switchers, whizzers
   drinkers out of scissors
   weave a tiny unit
   kids clemming in it
Piping in tizzes
two fight off one
even one eagle
   little gun swingers
   rivertop ringers
   one-name-for-all
   whose lives flow by heart
   beyond the liver
   into lives of a feather
Wag it here, Willy
pretty it there
flicker and whirr —
if you weren't human
how many would care?

Sandstone Country

Bush and orchard forelands stop sheer
with stencilled hands under mossed cliff eaves
and buried rain peeing far down off balconies
stains ink-dark and slows into leaves.

Blued biscuit towers, propped mile-high in screes
of petrified surf. Spear-carrying trees
crowd up there round lintels rolled from caves
above cornstalk farms with iron-hooped graves

Bleached rusting country, where waterfalls
reanimate froth and stripped-out cars
in hills being cleft for shopping malls.
If sex and help never dawned on Mars

maybe they're unique, and yet to spread
and Sun and Moon and barren stars
revolve round the scrub Earth after all,
pale handprints climbing an old smoked wall.

Manners of the Supranation

Along our hills, before the first star
arises the glow of Meruka,
the clearer, brighter, more focussed nation
we enter to rest from contemplation.

There songs are for watching, and sexy as war
and truth is what there is footage for.
Most death is by contract, though. And people kiss a lot
but reproduce by zoom and gunshot.

Night and Day are lighting terms. There are no cycles.
Seasons and epochs there are locales.
Breasts and faces are matte. Chests and horses shine
and everything spoken is a line

and actorly spoken — though in sport, men, not women
may talk like blokes. The lit bowl all swim in
streams fact, the shortest urban myth:
cholesterol, radon, IQ, coprolith.

Square-muscled as chocolate bars, sirens give tongue
but their fountain of youth is just for the young.
The authentic, from hoeing dry earth to raise rent,
stare into the wash cycle where their children went.

Very few are fat there; all are reduced;
poverty looks applied when it is produced.
The red neck, in country that never gets dark,
is curbed by young nobles from the National Park.

Labour's dim-sacred, business sinister, trade sly:
the only chic enterprise is private eye.
There the one book in everyone is filmed and on show
but its strange truths are trimmed to what viewers may know;

in spy series, the knowing may rise to despair
which is noblest and deadliest, above savoir faire.
Also Meruka loves animals, but hers have no smell
so those in the animal world can't tell,

but ads shine through satire like poems through critique
and to win on the replay is mortal technique
as, name-starred, the monolith from 2001
lies half sunk at right angles in Washington.

Meruka, death's babysitter, hearth fire of cool
the ads are in Hamlet and he's in Play School:
now you're First. Second's us, where we glance or lie curled,
and where anything still happens, that is the Third World.

High River
for the marriage of Brian and Mary Davis

We were all at the river before it was strange
and toddled to whoops all ribbed middays long
with sisters and kick-sprays, and the light came in tins
but, spilling or strapped up, love was there to soothe change.

Inside water all stayed, shaking; top stuff moved away.
The foggy telescoping cat who dreamed up from deep
was Yabbie, of crack forepaws, fond of waterlogged
      sandwich.
Turtles, finger-necked, pointed out "One regards one sky
      each."

Fringed eels, made all of tail, bumped a dog sunk in sleep
and the questioning length fathers shouldered to deep holes
jobbed, and wriggled up again, fixed through a dumb-
      shouting
kicker, in crisp saliva, who'd be sweet on sundown's coals.

The river swelled through concrete in cyclone-wire summers
and inside the greened rope-tree's palace of jerked m's.
It built bridges, teemed, raged brown miles wide to music;
one side was gorge and hidden — the same side was Thames.

One side was piano balcony, propelled by turning pages;
farther out, raging hulls cannonaded the linen trees.
Moved by fall but also rise to and far round the specific
the river was more illuminant than go by gravities.

      The words for field and coppice
      are knitted in our brains
      and yet the greening river
      is a tree-line on beige plains
      with biscuit precipices
      and clay-creamed chutes like drains

96

kinked outwards to rocket pipeclay
bums to a waterspout boom
out among squealing childhoods
that flash above a pernod gloom
bottles later will take some down to
away from the concrete room,
but it is our language dreaming
and not a bar of race
that what will still a crumbling
walled reach, and shade into place
is more likely than an iridescing serpent
to be a flagged, beamy space
stone-timbered, ringing and rapping,
barges with oars all aloft, stopping
and real water to every brim, lapping
not caked round roots, hiding its face.

In that water-meadow where punt-pole robots on red-
    tongued horses crash,
stag to martlets, before wowed women, bash, rocking, and
    counter-bash,
where running with wine and water-skins, servants fluster
    their final esses
and knights with faces paly wavy chain-boot their baggy
    fesses,

a table on edge has doorknob cups with wine in circular
    suspension;
behind it, twin abbeys seat a fair couple, each luminous with
    the other's attention.
Touching foods with one finger they hear bagpipes and a
    singer *Ayy Lucifer, come away:*
Lucifer-Exclusifer, sleeps with the torches lit, Lord of Darkness —
    by day.

The attended bishop from nuptial Mass is still diagonally
    departing
when a knight with appletree helmet rides up, his sunbright
    steels fitting and starting.

His horse looks where he speaks; he plants a sleeved lance;
    it too bears fruit and green leaves,
then, as a share stays in earth while blunt-pointed, but gets
    worn sharp and upheaves,

from a furrow of river half-crossing the scene there bursts a
    mighty fish.
"Gentle lady, gentle sir, we are here to answer any question
    you may wish,
for I, I know everything —" *And so do I, but I know it
    differently —*
"That is our limitation; now, the pair of you —" (*Your
    pardon, I see three.*

"You're counting their love? That's the pearl in which they
    move —" *No, thegn:*
*and ageless child holds their hands, the one no mortal child
    can remain.*)
"Happy pair, is there anything you would know this day?"
    They smile, and at minutely
separate moments, signify no. Warrior and fish exult mutely.

If they had needed lightest addition, or assurance from
    outside rapport,
perspective would have stripped the table, the Industrial Age
    started with a roar.
"Odd stuff, omniscience, Fish." *Yes. Plato's keeps guard
    dogs. Kung-fu, his sets an exam.*
"How many pinheads will that angel make dance?" *Just two
    characters in gravity dam?*

Helipterum Senecio Brachycome Minuria — crazy
the blessing we got from endless lake-floors of daisy
alone, and yellow-top, poverty bush, pink feather-dusty
    mulla mulla;
the floods spread from their rivers chrome and tan, but
    re-establish colour
in their absorption. The azure water dragon who sustains
most of our nation with cloud and green wrinkles and rains

crawled well to the east, by this time, of our speeding car
as we camped in isolation and drank at the odd isobar.
It was there, before Dodonaea and Sturt's Desert Pea
on a sun-splintered wharf a man said Newlyweds? Be
    happy.
A generation, at last, with no war at all in view;
jets parked with cockpits back, headless. What will we do
with all that human energy, if we've really drained the
    dragon?
Capital works are out, Identity's near exhausted, Space
    eats bone . . .
Build a freshwater river round the whole Pacific rim? It's
    been done
lately, and long ago. There's really only nurture and
    perversity.
Has the miracle come, the full stop of peace? To hope so is
    sound —
but bad and unwritten poetry do make the world go round
and God, to save your freedom, must only be privately
    found.
Had you noticed the world emptying even as it fills up?
Megacities, dying towns. This port ran its own Gold Cup,
now it runs only down. Under the rule of the Horse
people lived everywhere, by ignorance, by loyalty, by
    force.
Walled towns seemed better cover when the Hounds took
    over, of course,
but under the Hunt — you know, from first come-on
to pitying looks, that moment of life bounded by scorn? —
Province and Hinterland came back, in a re-run of Greece
    and Rome:
the sheer forgetting the wild Hunt requires can't afford
    accurate Home.
Economics? No, trade follows the poem. Work pays for
    fun —
so why keep them far apart? Turnover is production.
Communications? Indeed! What message did they ever
    send
but where the action is? And oh, contempt did not end.

What makes us young makes you old! The Hunt motto is
    distressing.
If your marriage disavows that, *it* is the peace. Take a
    madman's blessing!
Though the Darling Lily hitches its bulb ever deeper down
in the fox-coloured alluvium there, we left that town
for eye-crinking seas of Disphyma, quandong trees and
    native orange,
and where mansions are vacuumed out underground,
    beyond coherent drainage,
came where water drew shapes within shapes, as it
    relinquished spread.
Myriocephalus Dampiera O Solanum armatum, we said.

    Where river re-emerges
    confluent from dark
    it suckles like babies
    it rattles like work.

    Mine followed its own shape
    its glitter like the flat
    of the sword of landscape
    and took with ebullience

    enhancement from great rivers
    of Asia, of Europe,
    Callisto and California
    which swirl in reverse.

    Scrolling with energies
    or deep as soul-shiver
    in our climate you can
    get ahead of a river

    An oncoming semillon
    disc haloed like a star
    with paddock and rainforest
    where my people are

their knocked logs a gamelan
to the flute of ever-blue.
Within the water's cliff-face
men rotated and fish too

round a winding central axis
a thread I deeply knew
was woven of its edges.
The great fish could only chew

speech-bubbles now, being
in its legendary element
behind a sheerest curtain
yet though I stood perceiving

the line's long ascent
destroying plains to mountains
and back — each stage looked right —
on through life to my life

my mind rang with a wroth shout:
*How dare you be receiving
this vision without your wife?*
and I ran, and lost the image

till I saw it flow again
from her pen, as she sat jotting
under snapshots, the names slotting
with both spread and lineage

and in my great dread
of the departing river
I drew strength from her knowledge
that our centre is our edge.

Why give rhyme?
It could suggest that marriage itself is old-time.
Since we were hatched out of the crystal Spheres
and real and radio artillery entrenched a Big Bang in our ears

haven't we inhabited a hard knock in velocity
too serious with atrocity
to put the fact that one word looks brother to some other
    when heard
on a footing with high logics that make all seeming stability
a void demeaned by scrutability?

Love never gave up rhyme;
its utter re-casting surprises never found a kindlier mime.
I am listening now to women who from brew and bouillon
    of old caste
hoist up on soda-gnawed dowels the huge coiled cloths of
    the past
crying Who didn't know the cobbles might glimmer out at
    nothingness?
Of you, the best knew that gravity from underneath isn't
    levity
but when you were called from broad pleasing and required
    to impress
you sacrificed rhyme, the lovelier proof that impoverished
    less,
that added, and skip-turned, and added, on over the abyss.

Cool music of the synthesizer lengthens phrase as it loosens
    from earth,
it loses stress as breath and dance are jettisoned: it becomes
    a radiance-girth,
a shell of potencies expanding from one blinding source —
who in gravity must be citizen and deal with human
    difference.
One alone is mighty to create from; so is observation
but rhyme even in language is infinite, at maddening rich
    random, through dilation
faster ever than dictionaries. Never despise those
who fear an order vaster than reason, more charming than
    prose:
splendid lines may write themselves blank. But blest
surely are those who unknowingly chime with the noblest
and love and are loved by whom they rhyme with best.

So let your river be current and torrent and klong
as far and intricate as your love is long

(Cowan-Davis? Good heavens, that's the family we give
thanks to for Christmas. They made the Absolute our
    relative).

Myriad floating islands, each a ship of rules
enforced with a frown, a gritting of wrapped tools:

that billionaire's, who rebuilt charm downstream of his city
and imprisoned a Van Gogh for being richer than he,

the dying totalitarian twentieth century mind
turning in turn to wilderness, telling us what we must find,

the brown drift and fall of derelicts, playing deciduous
    parts
where the dancing Aztecs sing Uh-huh! Uh-huh! from their
    hearts.

Bad islands when they sink go down dry. They do not
    drown
but lie within water-walls you can't see from them,
    immeasurably down.

From them, it's hard to glimpse the lift or desperate rowing
    climb
of a few up fluid cliffs, out of their atmosphere, their time.

Your high level sailing draws up many. It is an aptitude
rather like an evergreen fig tree photocopying its food

or the close releasing arms that let a small child find its
    depth
back where your godfather on stepping stones rockingly
    stepp'th.

May the present still be your gift and the future ripe fruit
when I and (it happens) many relatives have become
    absolute.